BRANCH GROUPS

Covenant Discipleship for Youth

Lisa Grant

DISCIPLESHIP RESOURCES
MATERIALS FOR GROWTH IN CHRISTIAN FAITH AND LIFE

P.O. Box 189 • Nashville, TN 37202 • Phone (615) 340-7285

Also available from Discipleship Resources

Accountable Discipleship, by David Lowes Watson

The Early Methodist Class Meeting, by David Lowes Watson

Covenant Discipleship Member's Kit

Covenant Discipleship Congregation Kit

Youth Servant Team Handbook

United Methodist Youth Fellowship Handbook

Library of Congress Catalog Card No. 88-72383

ISBN 0-88177-067-1

DR067B

Contents

Introduction

Jesus said, "I am the true vine, and my Father is the vinedresser. Every branch of mine that bears no fruit, he takes away, and every branch that does bear fruit he prunes, that it may bear more fruit. You are already made clean by the word which I have spoken to you. Abide in me, and I in you. As the branch cannot bear fruit by itself, unless it abides in the vine, neither can you, unless you abide in me. I am the vine, you are the branches. He who abides in me, and I in him, he it is that bears much fruit, for apart from me you can do nothing.

(John 15:1-5)

Jesus' time in this world was nearly over when he spoke these words to the disciples. He knew this, and in these few words he gave his disciples an analogy for spiritual growth and nurture. It is clear that Jesus did not see spirituality as an inwardly directed journey only. This would make our spirituality isolated and self-contained. No growth can come unless it bears fruit. The fruit of spirituality comes only as God thrusts us out into the world to live faithfully as Christian disciples.

The image of the fruitful branch is an appropriate example for youth who are joining a Branch Group. There is, today, a sincere and intense felt need for spiritual formation and discipleship. More than just knowing about the faith, we need to *live* the faith. This need arises in various arenas of the church, but nowhere is it more evident than among some of our youth. Listen to your friends. Some are asking the weightier questions of faith. Some are attuned to the struggles of persons suffering from the effects of injustices in many parts of our world. Some are frustrated with a lack of straight talk about how to live as faithful Christians at school, at home, and at work. Some are tired of not having a place to share their concerns about the future. They know about teenage pregnancies, cocaine, AIDS, the debate on U. S. involvement in Central America, the struggle against apartheid, and the threat of nuclear annihiliation.

What is Christ calling you to do, and how can you find the courage to do it? How does faith bring meaning and help you make sense out of this complicated world?

1

The formula that we can follow to meet this need for a mature discipleship is set out clearly in the words of Jesus, in the image of the vine and the fruitful branches. The setting for putting this discipleship into practice comes from the basic organization of the early Methodist movement as set forth by John Wesley. He called it "the class meeting."

We are grateful for the work of David Lowes Watson, author of *Accountable Discipleship* (Nashville, TN: Discipleship Resources, 1984; order #DR009B). His work has made Wesley relevant for adults today. His model, Covenant Discipleship Groups, based on the early Methodist class meeting, is being used to revitalize hundreds of United Methodist congregations across this country. It is our prayer that Branch Groups for youth will be as fruitful.

Chapter One

Being a Disciple

Our world is a confusing and complex place. Living life in a fulfilling and meaningful way is a great challenge. It is not easy for adults and it is no easier for the youth of today.

In the personal realm there are important questions regarding your future. Will I go to college? What kind of career will I pursue? Who will my friends be? What activities will receive my time and energy as I establish life priorities? Sometimes your personal life is plagued with crises, big and small. Issues of divorce, illness, teenage pregnancy, drug and alcohol abuse, and even death can come frighteningly close to those for whom we care.

For many youth the world is a place overwhelmed with problems. You wonder how and even if you can make a difference, or if living is just a matter of survival. Unemployment and economic problems have affected your communities, your families, and your future. The possibility of nuclear war threatens this generation's sense of safety and security like no other generation before them. Are you helpless in the struggles for world peace?

The tasks of adolescent development are not easy under the best of conditions. What is important to me? What are my strengths and weaknesses? Do my friends like me? Even more important, do I like me? Where can I succeed? How do I cope with disappointments? All the issues of identity and intimacy converge on you, and it is not easy.

Jesus for Today

With different details, the same challenges were present two thousand years ago for the people of Jesus' day. "Follow me," Jesus said. The invitation was simple, straightforward, and direct. Simon Peter, James,

3

and John, the fishermen, left their nets and followed (Luke 5:1-11). Levi the tax collector left his office and everything behind (Luke 5:27-28). Crowds gathered to hear the good news and be healed from life's hurts. Jesus and his ministry touched them where they were with a message that was relevant for their life experiences.

The rewards for following were great. The poor heard good news. Freedom was announced to the prisoners. The blind received sight. The oppressed were released. This was God's time (Luke 4:18-21). Miracles happened, people were healed, and even sins were forgiven (Luke 7:48), for "the kingdom of God has come near" (Luke 10:11b).

But even in following, there were difficulties. Jesus also said that if persons came to him but put their family and friends and even their life before God, they could not be his disciples. To follow Jesus called for carrying one's own cross daily, experiencing denial of self and giving up one's own life priorities in order to find life (Luke 14:26-27; see also 9:23-27 and 9:57-62).

To those who would follow, Jesus offered salvation, wholeness, meaning, and fulfillment in life. He also challenged those who followed to live responsibly in community. He taught about a meaningful relationship with God the Father. He asked them to forgive one another, to love one another, to bring the kingdom close to others, and to serve, for what they did for another, they did for him (Matthew 25:34-41).

What Is a Disciple?

A disciple is one who follows another, usually as a student follows and learns from a teacher. But it is also going a step further. A disciple, in the best sense of the word, is one who accepts and assists in spreading the way of life of another.

Being a disciple of Christ has a purpose and a task. The first disciples were sent out as co-workers of Jesus with the mission to spread the message and the ministry of the kingdom to others. They were to cast out demons and cure diseases, to preach the kingdom of God and to heal the sick. It would not be easy. They were to take nothing with them on the journey, and they were being sent out like lambs among wolves. But Jesus had given them the power and authority needed for the task (Luke 9:1-6 and 10:1-12).

Being a disciple of Christ is both simple and complex. It is as simple as faith. It is as complex as life. It is more than learning a set of doctrines and beliefs. It is a way of living, a lifestyle. Being a disciple is more than learning or knowledge. It is more than knowing about the teacher, more than knowing about Jesus the Christ. It is being like Jesus. In Paul's words, it is having Christ formed in us (see Galatians 4:19). "How great . . . are the riches of the glory of this mystery, which is Christ in you" (Colossians 1:27).

Faith in Jesus Christ is opening ourselves to the life-changing and life-giving power of that living Christ as we confront all the complexities of our life. It is also living responsibly in the world as we are faithfully obedient to God's standards for the kingdom. It is a lifestyle of forgiveness and reconciliation, love and justice, righteousness and wholeness. Faith changes lives and transforms society.

To truly be a disciple, we must hold before us the balance of a gospel that both comforts and challenges. The good news of Jesus Christ comforts us when we are afflicted with the difficulties of life. That same gospel also afflicts us when we are comfortable. There is a world out there that needs to hear the message of Jesus Christ. God has chosen to use us, imperfect vessels that we are, to help bring the kingdom of God on this earth. That kingdom is brought close to another of God's children through each one of us, through our hands and feet and ears and lips and hearts of compassion. It is caring about the oppression and hunger and injustice and sickness of others simply because they are children of God. It is a caring that leads us to action on behalf of another, even entering into their suffering with them. This is the meaning of discipleship.

As living life is not easy, so is living life as a Christian not easy. We fool ourselves when we think the world is a friendlier place when we are Christian. Being a disciple in the fullest sense puts us right in the center of an unfriendly world. Sometimes as Christians we experience bumps and bruises from life in this unfriendly world. Living faithfully means living by a set of values and principles not always reaffirmed by the world. The world would teach us to live selfishly, doing what is best for me first. The world would encourage us to be expedient. Whatever is the easiest, the quickest, the least energy-spending is often what the world would teach us to do.

A Methodical Disciple

John Wesley, founder of the Methodist Movement over 200 years ago, knew the difficult challenge of living, particularly living as a Christian. He addressed the challenges with his General Rules for the United Societies. His model for living as a disciple was rooted in the early Methodist class meeting. Wesley prided himself in a Christianity that was practical with a faith that would speak in a plain and relevant fashion to the issues of real life. His model is still relevant today for United Methodists of all ages. Dr. David Lowes Watson of the General Board of Discipleship of The United Methodist Church has written a book, *Accountable Discipleship,* introducing the early Methodist class meeting to United Methodism today as Covenant Discipleship Groups.

If you are to be and become faithful disciples of Jesus Christ with all that discipleship means, support and guidance needs to be given. The Branch Group approach is a vehicle also based on the early class meeting whereby youth can receive the tools necessary to be faithful disciples.

Chapter Two

Building Discipleship

Most readers of this book know what it means to be Christian. We know the basics of faithful living. The real problem is in the actual obedience to these principles. We have at least the basic ideas of *what* we are to do, but we lack the *how*. How do we find the courage to follow when something else would be easier? How do we find the strength to do the right and Christ-like thing when something else would be easier? How do we know what God would have us do when all around us the voices of our culture tell us to watch out for ourselves first? How do we act in such a way as to make a difference in a world so dominated by conditions that are contrary to God's rule on earth? How do we avoid being overwhelmed and even immobilized by the huge problems of this world?

Practice

"Anything worth accomplishing is worth working for." That was the wisdom of my grandmother. That wisdom kept me going when I wanted to be a musician. As student director of our high school marching band, I grew to hate those hot, long practices that dared to interrupt my summer vacation. But the desire to be a good band was not enough. We had to work at it. We had to practice the same drills over and over again. Just because we had mastered them the day before, did not mean we could skip practice today.

Arthur Rubinstein, the famous pianist, once posed the riddle, "If I miss them one day, I know. If I miss them two days my teacher knows. If I miss them three days, the audience knows. To what do I refer?" The answer: practicing the scales.

There are certain practices of the Christian lifestyle that should be practiced each day if we are to become faithful disciples. No matter how mature we become in the faith, these are the same practices that will keep us in shape. We may never reach perfection, but we will not make any progress unless we practice. To be a Christian disciple we must practice Christianity. The desire is not enough. It takes hard work.

Discipline

A recent movie, *Hoosiers,* depicts a basketball coach's struggle to develop a winning team. As talented as the players may be, the first thing the coach does is to make the team run laps around the court. A winning team must be disciplined in the basics of the game. Sometimes we want to be winners for God, but we aren't even in shape at the most elementary level. We want to do God's will and be effective disciples, but we do not even know God's basic expectations as contained in the scriptures. We want to be effective players when we have not mastered the fundamental breathing skills of the game. We want to feel close to God, but we only communicate with God when there is a pinch in our lives. We want to change the social ills of our complex global world, but we can't even figure out what God would do in the everyday moments of our lives.

The goal is important, but if we are going to win we need to get in shape and stay in shape. There are certain disciplines of life that are as essential to our spiritual health as proper diet, rest, and regular exercise are to the physical health of the most gifted athlete. The early Methodists called these basic spiritual disciplines "the means of grace," and we will explore them in detail later.

Patience

Much attention has been given in recent years to the ill effects of television on all of us. One of the greatest disservices of situation comedies is that they lead us to believe that any and all of our problems can be solved in 30 minutes. Not only that, we can laugh all the way. Real life isn't like that.

We live in an instant society: instant milk, instant pudding, frozen dinners. Tap the microwaves and zap instant supper. Lotteries teach us to dream of instant wealth. Have an ache or a pain? Swallow pills promising instant relief.

There is no such thing as instant spirituality or instant discipleship. It takes hard work, practice, and patience. Being a disciple is a process of becoming a disciple. It is a process of living. First we learn. Then we put into practice in the everyday moments of life what we have learned. Maturing in faith and faithfulness takes a lifetime of living. We must be patient.

Community

How many times does being a Christian seem difficult because you feel as if you are alone? Sometimes when you look around it appears as though you are the only one trying to do what God might have you do. In a world where most people are looking out for themselves, to care for someone else makes us feel as though we are from another planet. The rugged individualism of American life stresses doing things by oneself and in one's own way. This can leave you isolated and lonely.

Most tasks in life are made easier when they are done in the company of another. Homework actually becomes fun when we study in a group. Doing the dishes is faster if I talk on the phone. One spring, as it came time to choose my summer camp experience, I decided to be adventuresome. I would go on a trail ride on horseback into the Allegheny Mountains. We would leave camp on Monday morning and not return until Saturday morning. All we could take with us had to fit rolled up in our bedding and tied onto the back of our saddles. We would ride for about six hours each day, cook over an open fire, and sleep under the stars. Fortunately 14 other teenagers had the same crazy idea as I. Without the support of each other and our counselors, we each would have given up and headed for civilization before Tuesday! We needed each other for encouragement. We did not know each other when we arrived on Sunday. By Wednesday we thought we had known each other all of our lives. We had become a community.

The disciples were a community. The first Methodists were a community. Being a disciple is eased by the fellowship and support of others who share our own joys and frustrations. We need to find and spend quality time with others who share our desire for discipleship.

Chapter Three

The Early Methodists

In the mid 1700s, amidst the struggles of the industrial revolution in England, a small band of preachers under the leadership of John Wesley moved throughout the countryside preaching a gospel of grace and practical Christianity. They came to be known as Methodists, for the method of discipleship they practiced.

Wesley was a son of a priest in the Church of England and was himself a pastor in that same church. Wesley desired in his ministry to bring new interest and vitality to the religious life of his day. As a student at Oxford University he and his brother Charles and several of their friends had joined together as a "Holy Club." They would rise early each morning for prayer and study together, practicing a disciplined life of discipleship. Between classes they would serve their neighbor by caring for the poor of London. These disciplines gave Wesley the foundations of what it meant in Paul's words to "work out your own salvation" (see Phillipians 2:12). But it was in 1738, when he returned from missionary work in Georgia, that he came to see *why* these disciplines were important. One evening at a Religious Society meeting in Aldersgate Street in London, Wesley was overwhelmed with the insight that God loved not just people in general but that God loved him, John. This time of personal insight he later described as having his heart strangely warmed, and we know it today as his Aldersgate experience.

Soon after this experience, Wesley began preaching around the countryside. He discovered that if the message of the gospel was to be heard by folks, he had to go to where they were. So he began to move about from village to village preaching at various times during the day wherever he could gather a group together. This style of field preaching quickly took hold.

As Wesley recruited other preachers and the Methodist Movement grew, the time came to organize. The result was the formation of the early Methodist class meetings. A class meeting was a weekly gathering

10

of about twelve persons who talked of their daily experiences as Christians, giving an account of their faithfulness and watching over one another in love. The meetings were led by a leader who, in addition to taking offerings to support the movement and taking attendance for the purpose of distributing class tickets, would encourage and admonish the members for their increased faithfulness.

Some say this model of organization was the very genius of John Wesley and the very backbone of the Methodist Movement. For a more complete understanding of the class meeting in its historical and theological setting, one should become familiar with two books by Dr. David Lowes Watson, *Accountable Discipleship* and *The Early Methodist Class Meeting*. Both are available from Discipleship Resources. An additional resource (also from Discipleship Resources) that will help explain the teachings of the early Methodist Movement is *Wesley Speaks on Christian Vocation*, by Paul Wesley Chilcote.

The class meeting existed to equip the members for Christian discipleship, particularly in a world that was hostile to the message of Jesus Christ. These early Methodists took seriously their call to go into the world through their daily lives and join God already at work in proclaiming the message and meaning of salvation. They readied themselves for this task with the practicing of several time-tested disciplines, which they came to know as the means of grace. It was through these disciplines that they received the power and form of God's grace to perform the tasks of discipleship. In the community of the class meeting, they could receive comfort and strength from one another as they shared the victories, the bumps, and the bruises of the difficult challenge of being a disciple in a less than friendly world.

In any edition of the *Discipline of The United Methodist Church*, under the section Historical Documents, the General Rules of the United Societies can be found. Ask your pastor for a copy. Written there can be found, in Wesley's own words, the purpose of the class meeting as well as the building blocks needed in everyday living for those early Methodists to be faithful disciples.

Means of Grace

Methodists were called to
1. Do all the good they could for God and their neighbor.

   2. Avoid doing harm to God and their neighbor.
   3. Avail themselves of the means of grace.

The means of grace were understood to be these disciplines:

   1. Daily prayer
   2. Daily study of the Bible
   3. Weekly worship
   4. Receiving of the sacraments
   5. Fasting and temperance
   6. Stewardship of one's resources
   7. Christian fellowship where conversation about one's faith journey could occur

We find in John Wesley's theology a strong emphasis on an understanding of grace. By grace we are given possibility of faith (prevenient grace) in God. By grace we are saved from our sins (justifying grace). By grace we are made perfect or mature in our discipleship (sanctifying grace). God's grace or loving kindness is active in every moment of life. That grace is drawing us, luring us, prompting us to be and act according to the Divine Will. Obedience to such gracious nudges of God cannot be neglected for one moment.

For Wesley the assurance of faith is not what saves us from sin. Sometimes we know what we believe and are convinced to the point of absolute certainty about it. At other times we are filled with doubts and questions. Wesley himself had questions and doubts less than a year later about his own experience at Aldersgate Street. Therefore, for Wesley, even if one was not absolutely sure of faith in God, one still needed to participate in some practical actions of life that were examples of Christianity. For Methodists, the separation of faith and good works is impossible.

In the early Methodist class meeting the common thread among the participants was not the experience of faith. It was rather the desire for faith. Regardless of the experience, the age, the language used, even the intellectual and emotional assurance of faith, the lifestyle to be pursued was and is the same. The factor which brings your branch group together is the practice of doing good, avoiding harm, and the practice of the means of grace.

These disciplines were not and are not salvation by good works. We are saved by grace. By grace God takes the initiative, by grace we respond, and the result is a new relationship with God. These disciplines are not the end. They are only the means to an end, a means to the grace of God. The question is this: How do we open ourselves to grace that we may experience the comfort and receive the strength and power needed for the difficult challenges of life? How does God work grace in us so that we grow, mature, and increase in our faithfulness as disciples of Jesus Christ?

Wesley found the answer in the class meeting, where persons could be mutually accountable for their discipleship. For adults today in The United Methodist Church the answer is a Covenant Discipleship Group. For youth the answer is the Branch Group.

Chapter Four

Branch Groups:
Class Meetings for Youth

A Branch Group is a group of six to eight youth and one adult who agree to meet together weekly and watch over one another in love. They report to each other their joys and struggles with living faithfully as Christians in today's world. They write a covenant of mutually acceptable disciplines which they agree to follow individually, in order to get in shape and stay in shape as disciples. With the fellowship of each other, they will experience community, exercise patience, and practice the disciplines that are essential for growing discipleship.

They have agreed to meet together for one hour each week. They have covenanted together for a twelve-week period, after which the covenant is renegotiable. The practical questions of the content of the covenant, the weekly meeting, the recruitment process, and questions of leadership will be addressed later.

Branch Groups are based on, and adapted from, the early Methodist class meeting model of John Wesley. The larger purpose of the Branch Group is the developing of those basic building blocks needed by all Christians for spiritual formation. Developing such discipleship happens best when you share your life together rather than as individual and isolated Christians.

Branch groups can be better understood if we see what they are not. They are not Bible study groups. They are not prayer groups. They are not sharing/caring groups. Each of these has its place and purpose within your church.

Branch Groups are accountable discipleship groups. They have an agenda to follow the agreed upon covenant. The items of the covenant are of mutual agreement to every member of the group. The items of the covenant help you walk in faithful discipleship (as understood in our first chapter). Finally, the process of accountability is the method which makes the group work each week. Youth can best support other youth in this process. The mutual accountability of the Branch Group is not judgment, it is the kind of loving support that reinforces spiritual formation.

We best exercise discipline, even when dealing with matters of faith, when we are accountable to others, that is when you are watching over me in love and I am watching you. Accountability is a vital element of Branch Groups. We are accountable for our discipleship, for practicing the disciplines that build discipleship, and for the fruit of our discipleship as we live in the world.

Accountability has another source as well. Accountability to members of a Branch Group is not enough in and of itself. We are also accountable to the Holy Spirit. The dynamic of God's grace working in and through us cannot be overlooked or taken for granted. The primary focus of Branch Groups is not accountability to each other. The primary focus is not even the disciplines themselves. The primary focus is God. It is God who calls us into discipleship. Through these time-honored disciplines we believe that God fills us with love and grace. It is God who moves us beyond concern for ourselves to mission and ministry to others around us. It is God who gives the gifts and the graces needed to respond to the hurts of the world. God chooses to use us to make a difference in the world by compassionately fighting against the causes of the suffering. It is God who unites us together as we support one another in Branch Groups. It is God who effects change in each participant as we grow in our maturity as Christians. It is God who forms Christ within us. All we do is make ourselves available to God.

Hold before your group the image of the vine and the branches. Remember that the group is only a channel of God's grace. The focal point must be God. It is God who will bring about change and growth in the individuals, the group, the congregation in which you serve, and the world. Participation in and of itself does not guarantee change. Branch Groups simply provide a setting in which each member can practice actively the disciplines of discipleship and receive encouragement from one another. This is important for the group's perception of its role in implementing the will of God and furthering the ministry and love of Christ Jesus. Through the group, members may become increasingly open and receptive to God's grace and thus be transformed by God in the very midst of the complexity, hardship, and confusion of their day-to-day lives.

Chapter Five

The Covenant

Welcome to your Branch Group! You and several other youth have covenanted together to hold one another accountable for your discipleship. The disciplines of your discipleship will be defined in the writing of and agreeing upon a covenant.

The early Methodists agreed to adhere to the General Rules of the Methodist societies as their covenant. These rules had three major components: using the means of grace, avoiding wrong, and doing good. The means of grace were approved by the church and had been proven in practice. They were listed as follows:

1. Prayer (private, family, and public)
2. Searching the scriptures
3. The sacrament of the Lord's Supper
4. Public worship
5. Fasting
6. Christian fellowship

These works of piety were ways in which God's grace was brought to them. But just as a body of water that has an inlet and no outlet becomes dead and stagnant, so must there be a way in which the grace flows through us to the world. Thus the general rules also included the works of mercy summarized as 1) Not to sin against God and one's neighbor, and 2) To do all the good one can for God and one's neighbor.

A covenant has three basic parts: the body which contains the specific clauses of agreement, a preamble, and a conclusion. The preamble states the purpose for creating the covenant. The conclusion focuses the dominant focal point of the covenant.

Following is a sample covenant:

MY BRANCH GROUP COVENANT

Knowing that Jesus Christ died for me and that God calls me to be a disciple of Jesus Christ, I desire to practice the following disciplines in order that I might know God's love, forgiveness, guidance, and strength. I desire to make God's will my own and to be obedient to it. I desire to remain in Christ with the help of this covenant so that I might bear fruit for the kingdom of God.

1. I will pray each day.
2. I will read the Bible each day.
3. I will worship each Sunday, unless prevented.
4. I will avoid doing those things which I know will cause me or someone else harm in any way.
5. I will do those things which serve God by being helpful to others.
6. I will attend the weekly Branch Group meeting where I will give an account of my efforts to keep this covenant. By the fellowship of this group I will be strengthened and will be supportive of the other members of my group.

I make this commitment trusting God's grace to work in me. If I fail in my efforts I will trust God's grace to forgive me and help me that I would have the strength to grow in my faith.

Date_____ Signed_____

This sample covenant represents the essential core clauses of any Branch Group covenant. The first task of a newly formed Branch Group is the writing of the covenant. The preamble and the conclusion may be creative pieces that fix the purpose of the covenant (the preamble) and focus the covenant process on God (the conclusion). The six core clauses may be adjusted in wording to fit the specifics of each group situation, but all six core clauses should be included in some fashion. These six core clauses are a necessary part of the covenant of every Branch Group. It is the foundation upon which the entire program is based. The omission of any one of these individual elements from a covenant would compromise the integrity and effectiveness of the entire Branch Group concept.

Core Clauses

Let's examine these core clauses to better understand their significance. Several other resources may be helpful in regard to these and other disciplines. *Celebration of Discipline,* by Richard J. Foster, was published in 1978 by Harper & Row and is available from your local bookstore. *Devotional Life in the Wesleyan Tradition,* by Steve Harper, was published in 1983 by The Upper Room and is available from The Upper Room. Also published by and available from The Upper Room are several workbooks by Maxie Dunnam. Of particular help is his *Workbook on Spiritual Disciplines.* Also extremely valuable are the two books by Dr. David Lowes Watson, *Accountable Discipleship* and *The Early Methodist Class Meeting,* and the book *Wesley Speaks on Christian Vocation* by Paul Wesley Chilcote, all published by and available from Discipleship Resources.

Prayer

Thousands of books have been written regarding prayer, including those that inspire it, those that broaden our understanding of it, and those that seek to increase both the quantity and quality of our prayer lives. For our purposes, three basic things need to be mentioned about prayer in your covenant.

First, most persons think of prayer as conversation with God. In one sense this is true. Prayer is about learning that we can communicate fully, openly, and honestly with God about anything and everything. We need not hold anything back, including our darkest emotions. The honesty of the psalmist teaches us this kind of frank prayer. We must also remember that good communication is a two-way street. Not only do we need to grow comfortable in expressing ourselves to God, we also need to learn how to quietly wait and listen to God in the silence of reflective and meditative times.

Second, we are told to make our requests known to God. Most of us do not understand fully how prayer works. Jesus made requests to God and taught us to do so as well. The important thing is that we develop a rhythm about our prayer life that encourages a balancing of many types of prayer: adoration, confession, petitions for ourselves and for others, and thanksgiving.

Last, many important things have been written, particularly the spiritual classics of Christianity, that help us strengthen and deepen the level of our prayer life. Paul teaches us to pray constantly. Prayer at its deepest level is being in the presence of God, allowing God to form the Christ within us. It is prayer that transforms us. It is by prayer that we are known by God and come to know God. Prayer of this form is often prayer expressed through our actions. Those who marched for civil rights in the 1960s were said to have prayed with their feet. Two classics, *The Practice of the Presence of God* by Brother Lawrence and *The Testament of Devotion* by Thomas Kelly, are both helpful and appropriate for many youth of today. Another excellent resource for exposure to a variety of Christian classics is a collection by The Upper Room entitled *Selections from the Living Classics*. Whether you read these books or not, the bottom line is still this: Did you pray today?

Scriptures

Reading the Bible is difficult for many adults and youth. We need to find ways to make the Bible "user friendly." For this reason, suggestions for reading and studying are essential. The use of already designed daily lectionaries (specific Bible readings assigned for each day) and study books of common interest to the group is encouraged.

The highest authority of life is God's Word, the Bible. It is to be read daily. It is to be searched daily, searched because it contains truth and wisdom relevant to our own lives of discipleship. By the Spirit, God still uses the Bible to speak to us today. Our problem is that we have been so taught to read critically that we approach the scripture wrong from the beginning. In the best sense, the Bible should be read like a love letter. It can be read again and again and each time speak in a new way. Beginning our time with prayer can help us to be open to the Spirit's use of the Word for us.

In general, regardless of the passage being read, asking these four questions about the passage is helpful.

1. What was this passage about for the people of biblical times?
2. What does the passage mean for us today?
3. What is the passage saying to me right now?
4. What am I going to do about what this is saying to me?

You do not have to be a biblical scholar to find the Bible relevant for your life. If one translation is difficult to read, try another. Read systematically. Ask questions. Remember that you have a lifetime to read, so read with depth.

It is God's Word. God still uses it today to speak to us. Resolve to put what you read and learn into practice.

Worship

Corporate worship was important for Wesley because it connected the Methodist movement with the Church of England. It was in worship that the sacrament of Holy Communion was received and the Word of God was read and expounded upon.

Worship takes on the meaning it is intended to have if we remember why we worship. Some of us attend church hoping that the choir has a good performance and the sermon is interesting. We expect to be entertained. Actually we have the purpose mixed up. Worship is for God. God is the one for whom worship is being performed. The choir and the pastor are only helps for us in the congregation to act out our worship, our praise, and adoration for God. God is the audience, we are not. Worship is something we do for God because God is God and is worthy of our praise. Such praising of God is certainly a discipline of the Christian disciple.

Worship is also an occasion for re-focusing our lives on Christ as the Center. The Word read and preached can comfort and challenge us for a better understanding of the meaning of discipleship. Certainly God can and does speak to us as we worship.

Avoiding Harm

Today, just as in Wesley's day, Christians are tempted in a variety of ways to do that which they ought not do. Some things are to be avoided because they are harmful to our own well-being. Some things are to be avoided because they are harmful to others. God's Spirit is always at work in our lives, moment by moment, warning against that which is sin. Are we obedient?

This clause of your covenant provides you with the opportunity to reflect on and share your struggles and then say "NO." It may begin with not gossiping or saying hurtful things in the midst of an angry moment. It may lead to having the courage to stand up for what we believe is right even under the most intense of peer pressures. It may have to do with personal moral dilemmas, and it may even lead to discussion and action in regard to global issues of oppression and injustice. Sometimes the North American way of life contributes to an international process of doing harm to others, by encouraging the exploitation of Third World countries.

This clause introduces us to the dynamic way in which God, through the Spirit, interacts in the everyday situations of life. God's grace works at preventing us from sinning. Are we sensitive to that work and do we respond? We can begin to learn how to avoid harm of many magnitudes by wrestling with this clause.

Doing Good

As in scripture, Wesley believed that just to avoid sinning was not enough. We must take action to show love and compassion. To care for another was to serve God.

Doing good happens at two levels. First, realize that a lot of what we are taught as being polite and helpful is, if only in a small way, serving God. If the Spirit is active in every moment of life, our urges to do as we have been taught are promptings of the Spirit. We may begin by being sensitive to others around us and by being helpful in the seemingly little arenas of life.

Second, this heightened sensitivity to the Spirit's prompting in the everyday moments of life leads to sensitivity on a broader level. Soon we find ourselves sensitive to the needs and hurts of people very different from ourselves, even miles across the ocean. What are we being prompted to do for the hungry, the lonely, the outcast? How are we working for peace and justice?

Branch Groups, as they master the basics of the covenant, may find themselves being led to take on specific projects, individually or as a group, in response to this clause. A helpful resource for projects is the *Youth Servant Team Handbook* from Discipleship Resources.

Fellowship

Fellowship is more than socializing with friends in the Christian community. It is having serious conversation about matters of the faith. It is being able to share the stories of our own spiritual journey. It is being supported by others and offering support to others. In short, it is the quality of conversation necessary for a class meeting to serve its purpose. For Branch Groups to be effective, the same is true. Therefore, this clause is about being present and participating in the weekly Branch Group meeting.

The most important thing to remember about the core clauses is this: they are only disciplines that show you how to be open to the powerful and life-changing grace of God. Each discipline is only a building block for faith development. Use and understand them as such.

Additional Clauses

In addition to the necessary core clauses of the Branch Group covenant, there are two other kinds of clauses your group may wish to consider. The first is the **optional clause.** These are additional clauses that your entire group has agreed upon in order to address a specific need or concern. Here are a few suggestions that will help stimulate your own creativity:

1. I will journal three times a week.
2. I will participate in a community activity that serves people less fortunate than myself.
3. I will talk with someone each week about my experience of being a Christian.
4. I will participate in a weekly Bible study class.

John Wesley included fasting and receiving the Lord's Supper as means of grace. Because of eating disorders among teenagers, some groups today broaden this concept to include general concerns for healthy living and overall temperance. In groups that have been together for awhile, one might want to consider the addition of a clause along these lines, "Knowing that my body is a temple for the Holy Spirit, I will prayerfully care for my body."

Certainly the receiving of the Lord's Supper is as important a means of grace today as it was for Wesley's day. Communion is in a real and powerful sense food for our souls. As a sacrament ordained by God, it reminds us of God's love and forgiveness which are shown through the suffering, death, and resurrection of Jesus Christ. It also is a symbol of our unity with each other and God. Paul reminds us that we participate in the sufferings of Christ when we share the sacrament together (1 Cor. 10:16-17). Therefore the sacrament becomes an important part of the life of a Branch Group. Each group will have to determine how and if the receiving of the sacrament can be included in their covenant. The pastor could certainly be invited to serve the Branch Group Communion occasionally or regularly at its weekly meeting.

The concept of stewardship was also an important discipline for Wesley. The more advanced groups might want to think about clauses about ecology or stewardship in the broadest sense. "I will prayerfully care for the world in which I live." Some groups will want to include issues of financial stewardship such as, "I will use my financial resources prayerfully and carefully," or even "I will give a tenth of my income to the church."

The second kind of additional clause you might consider is the **open clause.** The open clause is to provide for an individual to make a personal covenant for which he or she will be accountable to the group at the following Branch Group meeting. Remember that the function of the group is always to enhance faithfulness. Sometimes an individual will need extra support in a given area of his or her life. Open clauses allow for flexibility and tailoring to the needs of individuals. Sue may need help resolving a conflict with a friend. Bill may need help being faithful in his study for an upcoming math test. Juan may need help remembering his chores. Carol may be wondering about volunteering at the nursing home and needs to be held accountable for finding out what is involved in such work. Each can be cheered on by fellow Branch Group members as they report back at the next meeting.

Writing the Covenant

A few words of caution are in order. Keep in mind the need for a balance between the idealistic and the realistic. The clauses need to reflect a stretching for growth as the members get in shape. If the expectations are too high, members will feel overwhelmed and the entire process will frustrate, rather than enhance, maturity. Individuals also need to believe that the goal of the covenant is attainable. In other words, don't let the covenant get too long or too complicated. On the other hand, don't let the group be too easy on themselves. Either extreme will defeat the motivation of the members as well as the overall goals of the Branch Group program.

Each clause of the covenant needs to be limited in scope and quite specific in its expectations. Your group should strive to reduce unclear clauses in order to minimize confusion among the members. This is important, both as they try to fulfill the covenant, and as they hold each other accountable each week.

For the beginning Branch Group, it is unlikely that the members will feel able to include anything in the covenant beyond the core clauses. Some Branch Groups may never add anything beyond the core clauses, no matter how long they meet. That's okay. Everyone needs to begin with basic training, and no matter how advanced we get in anything, certain practices need to continue, always and forever. Remember the pianist who still plays those same scales!

Whatever development your own Branch Group takes, remember the focus. The purpose is to enhance the spiritual development of youth by encouraging the disciplines of the Christian life. This is very straightforward, practical, and manageable.

Again, remember the uniqueness of the Branch Group. Don't confuse it then, either in the covenant itself or the meetings, with Bible study groups, prayer groups, sharing sessions for personal psychological growth, or social action and outreach groups. These are important aspects of ministry that must be taken care of in other arenas within the congregation. For example, if you form a *Youth Servant Team,* make it a separate endeavor from the Branch Group meeting. Branch Groups are for mutual accountability in regard to discipleship. Keep the focus clear, specific, and limited.

Signing the Covenant

Once the covenant is agreed upon by all members of the group, have the members sign the covenant. Some groups desire to have all the signatures on each one's individual covenant. This reminds them visually that they are in this together. It is helpful if the covenant can be carried with each member in a wallet or kept in his/her Bible.

There will be time every twelve weeks for the renegotiation of the covenant. It is recommended that no changes be made during each twelve-week period. It takes time and patience to become proficient at anything. Twelve weeks is the minimum time to live with a covenant before you know what needs to be adjusted. Re-covenanting is discussed in a later chapter.

Chapter Six

The Weekly Branch Group Meeting

It is in the weekly Branch Group meeting that the dynamic of accountability in the community of faith comes alive. What is experienced, learned, and felt by the participants in the weekly meeting will greatly influence the effectiveness of the Branch Group model.

First, let us review the overall plan. It is suggested that a group be formed and members covenant to meet together for an initial period of twelve weeks. During this first phase, the resources in the Appendix can be used to help the participants understand the broad purpose, philosophy, and interaction of the Branch Group process. Recommended Bible readings can be assigned for individual use in one's personal daily devotional time. Specific prayer suggestions may be made. This first twelve-week period is one of introduction to the foundational building blocks that help every Christian live as faithful disciples.

After the initial twelve-week period of introduction, the group is asked to re-covenant for an additional period of time. The actual time frame will vary from setting to setting. Ordinarily groups will re-covenant for a six- to nine-month period. A definite beginning and ending date should be established. At the end of that second phase, groups can re-covenant again. Re-covenanting can occur numerous times, but each phase should last at least three months. The process of re-covenanting is discussed later.

It is more realistic and beneficial for you to commit for a specified and limited time, rather than an open-ended, indefinite period. Although the disciplines that build strong disciples are disciplines to be followed for a lifetime, and although there is hope that some persons would hear the call to be a part of a Branch Group and then to be a part of an adult Covenant Discipleship Group, a defined and manageable period of time initially will make the process more appealing.

Each Branch Group should plan to meet once a week at a time that is mutually agreeable to everyone in the group. The group should agree to meet for 60 to 90 minutes. The length of each meeting should be determined and agreed to at the beginning of the covenant process. At first groups will probably need 90 minutes to include discussion of material helpful for the initial learning time. Obviously, the more participants in a group, the more time is needed for each to be in conversation about his or her own accountability.

Each Branch Group should also agree to meet at a location that is convenient for every member. Just as meeting at a regular time is essential, so is it essential to meet at a regular place each week. Meeting somewhere in the church building is probably best, as other settings can provide unwanted distractions.

Agenda

The agenda for each meeting is determined by the group's covenant. The following outline will help with the flow of the actual meeting.

1. Opening prayer by the leader or another member of the Branch Group.
2. Review the covenant either by reading it aloud or silently.
3. Reporting by the individual members, accounting for their actions regarding the covenant during the past week. Members are encouraged to share their successes and their difficulties at this time.*
4. If someone in the group has offered a personal open clause at the last meeting, give him/her an opportunity to report.
5. Ask if anyone has a personal open clause for which he/she wants to be accountable during the next week. (Make sure the leader keeps a record of these so as to ask for a report at the next meeting.)
6. Closing prayer led by the leader or another member.

The reporting process is central to the work of the group. This process is **not optional** and must be a part of every group meeting if the

---

*Since a Branch Group is just getting started, additional time should be taken to help fully understand the meaning and significance of each item in the covenant. Discussion of the suggested Bible readings for beginning groups (as found in the Appendix) should occur at this time.

Branch Group is to function effectively. It is the methodical side of the concept of accountability.

In reporting on covenant items, the leader will start with herself or himself and account for her or his actions with regard to the first item. The leader will then ask each member in turn for a similar accounting. Each item should be dealt with in turn, giving each person an opportunity to report on the given item before the group moves on to the next clause.

The leader must watch the clock, making sure that each person has time to report on a given clause. The leader will need to be sensitive to the amount of talking any one person does. By allowing one person to dominate a meeting, you will deny sufficient time to the other persons for their reporting. Should one person have a specific need or dilemma that he/she wishes to discuss at length with the group, the leader may suggest that the group agree to meet longer for that session and deal with the issue after the reporting of all the covenant has occurred.

Should the leader discover that for unforeseen or uncontrollable reasons, the group is running out of time before all has been reported, the following week's meeting should begin where the group left off the preceding week. The time it takes for reporting is a very real issue to consider when the group is deciding on additional items to be added at the time of re-covenanting.

During the reporting process, the leader and the other members of the group may make appropriate responsive comments to the reports of others. The care given, the tone of the interaction, is of utmost concern. **Accountability does not mean berating, scolding, criticizing, putting down, being vicious, or inflicting guilt.**

Appropriate comments are those that support and sometimes offer suggestions for improvement. Gentle challenging for moving someone along in discipleship must be done intentionally and carefully with great love. As such, responding requires wisdom and knowledge of each member as an individual. Suzie is sensitive and presently needs affirmation and understanding. Mary may be looking for practical suggestions for finding a time each day to do devotions. Bill is wrestling with the meaning of prayer and wants the input of the other members. Each requires a different response to benefit from accountability.

Necessary conversation has these general guidelines.

1. Accountability is not judging (Matt. 7:1-7 is helpful.)
2. Participants must not be forced to say more than what they desire to say. Questions can be asked, but the privacy of the individual is to be respected.
3. Listening actively is essential. Participants must feel heard.
4. Let the individual set the pace. The time will come when a member, if he/she is taking the Branch Group seriously, will want suggestions and help from the group in order to improve. Individuals, as they get to know one another, will invite the deepening of the conversation. Trust the group process.
5. Recognize that in every group there still exist personal relationships. What Mary can say to Beth without threatening her may be very different from what Bill can say to Beth without hurting her feelings.
6. When successes are shared, this is the occasion for thanksgiving and rejoicing. When failures are shared, this is a time to learn about forgiveness and to begin anew from that moment.

Ephesians 4:15-16 speaks of building up the body as we grow into Christ. Matthew 7:1-7 reminds us to be careful of seeing the speck in another's eye when we have a log in our own. The process of learning accountability is a process of learning what it means to live by these two images.

A Sample Conversation

LEADER: It's good to see you all again. Let's open with prayer. "God, we thank you for being with us this week. Be with us now as we share together. Help us to listen to each other and you as we take this time to consider how and when we have been faithful to our covenant." Amen.

Did you all remember the copy of our covenant? Let's take a moment and read it over.
(After some silence, he or she begins again.)

Okay, I'll begin with the clause about prayer. My prayer life was pretty good this week. I know I prayed in some fashion every day. There were, however, two days when my devotional time was rushed so that my prayer time got cheated. I wasn't always intentional about my intercessory prayers for others. I'm working on it, but it still needs to be improved. Juan, how about you? How was your prayer life this week?

JUAN: I guess I'll have to say it was inconsistent. Sometimes I pray in the mornings, but this week I got up late most mornings. Then I'd try to remember them at night and mostly I forgot. Once I remembered to do my devotions after school, but my brother kept bugging me.

LEADER: Juan, I think we can all relate to how hard it is to pray regularly every day. I guess that's why a regular time each day is important.

JUAN: Yeah, I think I'd do better if I set aside the same time every day. I'm going to try to find the best time to do this every day at the same time.

JOHN: I decided I'd do my prayers and Bible reading before I went to bed each night. This week I haven't done very well. I've had a lot of homework, and then I fall asleep without praying.

LEADER: It sounds like you've had a hectic week. Hopefully the next one will be better. Sue, how was your prayer life?

SUE: I don't know what to say. Mostly I guess I didn't pray except for grace at meals with Mom and Dad. I had a lot of tests this week. I asked God to help me learn the material while I was studying and then I asked for help before each test. I guess I talked to God but it wasn't much more than one sentence asking for help.

JOHN: That reminds me, are there different kinds of prayer? *(At this point the group discusses the different kinds of prayer. With the leader's direction they discover that some prayers are quick one-liners and at other times prayer is meditative.)*

BILL: Well, it doesn't matter how you look at it, I didn't pray this week except for one morning in the shower. I guess that's pretty bad, but praying is hard for me. I forget and if I remember, I don't know what to say. *(The group expresses understanding of this problem. Some share things they've learned in other settings about prayer.)*

LEADER: Bill, before you joined a Branch Group, did you pray at all?

BILL: No, except maybe when I had a real big problem.

LEADER: Then just the fact you're thinking about prayer is an improvement. It will get better if it's important to you. Lynn?

LYNN: Gee, I almost feel bad because praying comes easy for me. I prayed every day. It's just conversation with God. We talk about everything.

LEADER: Thanks, Lynn, you help the rest of us.

JUDY: Conversation, huh? I get so frustrated because my mind wanders. I guess nothing is inappropriate if I'm just sharing with God. In that case, I'll change my answer. I was going to say I didn't do very well because I'd start to pray, then my thoughts would go off in some other direction and then I'd remember minutes later that I was trying to pray.

LEADER: It takes time to focus one's prayers and to be silent long enough to enjoy the time spent in prayer. It sounds like we all have room for improving.

(The group moves on to the other areas of the covenant, moving more quickly with yes and no answers.)

LEADER: How about the clause about serving? Remember last week we had a rather lengthy discussion about this. Sometimes serving is just doing ordinary little nice things and sometimes it is a big noticeable thing. We agreed that this week we would try to be specific in our answers. Well, this week I got a call from the woman next door. I didn't really know her, but her refrigerator had broken down and she wanted to store some things in mine. I was going to be late to a meeting, but I told her she was welcome to the space, and I helped her carry the food over and put it in my refrigerator. *(The group begins to tease the leader, since he is single. After some time of joking, he settles them down and pulls the discussion back to the covenant.)*

LEADER: Okay. So how about the rest of you?

BILL: I want to go first because I have done so well with this one. My grandpa has come to live with us. He's had a stroke so he can't live alone, at least not right now. My mom is really worried about him. I have tried to be as helpful as I can around the house. Yesterday Mom thanked me.

LEADER: Bill, it's terrific that you have been willing to be so suppor-
          tive. We are sorry to hear about your grandfather, but it's
          wonderful that he can stay with you. You know, just a
          minute ago you said you hadn't prayed much this week.
          Bill, maybe you are learning to pray with your actions. We
          will all pray for you and your family, especially your grand-
          father.

JUAN: I'll go next. I didn't do anything out of the ordinary, but I
          am trying to get along better with my brother. This week
          my swim team lost. I went over and congratulated the guys
          that had beat me. That was hard. Do these things count?

LEADER: What do the rest of you think?

BILL: Yeah, I think they count. I thought we said this clause was
          about not just thinking about ourselves first.
          *(The group agrees with Bill and they share a little about
          how hard it is to be good sports when they lose.)*

LEADER: Okay, Lynn, how did you do this week?

LYNN: I guess I'm making a little progress. I didn't really do
          anything special, but now I know what serving means.
          Mostly at night I could think about the day and remember
          things I could have done.

LEADER: Praying comes so easy for you. Why don't you pray about
          this and ask God to help you recognize things you could do
          when you are actually in the situation? John . . .

JOHN: Well, this has been a really weird week. In current events
          class I got in a big debate with this kid about apartheid.
          We are studying South Africa. He said the United States
          shouldn't get involved with economic sanctions and stuff. I
          said we should. Last night at dinner, my older sister, who is
          home from college, was talking about how there are chil-
          dren in prison over there and there is a group on her
          campus that is raising money to help get them free. I wish I
          knew more about this.

LEADER: Sometimes our curiosity is a way God speaks to us. Maybe
          I can find some information on what the church is doing in
          South Africa. John, stop by the office tomorrow. Maybe
          there is some way you or we will want to get involved. You
          could report back to us next week.

JUDY: There is a new student in my English class. She sits beside me. I've been trying to make friends with her. That's all I've done to help anyone this week.

LEADER: And that is an important thing. Finally, Sue, you've not said anything.

SUE: I guess that's because I haven't done anything. I've just been so busy with the tests this week. Almost every night I've been studying with somebody. I haven't thought about anything but school.

LEADER: You studied with other people?

SUE: Yes.

LEADER: Didn't you help each other study?

SUE: Yeah.

LEADER: Well, Sue, serving is about doing what you can, where you can. Maybe it doesn't seem like much. Maybe it's not all you should be doing, but those everyday experiences are important just the same.

Well, our time is almost up. Since we are all in attendance tonight, we can all say "yes" to our clause on fellowship. John and I are going to do some investigating about South Africa. Are there any other open clauses?

JUDY: I really want to invite this new student to a party I'm going to this weekend. Will you ask me about it next week?

BILL: And I have a request. will you pray for my grandpa?

LEADER: Yes to both and let's close now with prayer.

"God, we thank you for each other. We have had some good times and some rough times this week. Where we have been less than you would want us to be, touch us with forgiveness. Help us to celebrate our victories and to try a little harder where we are lacking. We pray especially for Bill's grandpa. Be with him. Be with us all, through Jesus Christ. Amen."

Chapter Seven

Leadership

Initially the Branch Group should be led by an adult. The role of the leader is crucial during the meeting time. The leader is to structure and manage the agenda of the meeting. The leader sets the pace in the accountability process by sharing an account of his or her actions first. Most important, the leader must model appropriate responses for the members of the group as they report on their faithfulness to the covenant. When members of the group respond inappropriately to one another, it is the leader who must address the situation.

Later in the Branch Group process, a youth may emerge as a potential leader, to be chosen by the adult leader. Caution must be taken that such a peer leader is indeed respected and recognized by every member of the group. Even if a mature youth is given responsibility for leading a weekly meeting, the adult leader should still be present. Rotation between adult and youth leadership may be the best way to ensure that the focus and direction of the Branch Group is not lost.

The most important qualification of the adult leader of a Branch Group is a commitment to the development of the faith of youth. Obviously he or she must understand the value of developing certain disciplines as the building blocks needed for spiritual formation. He or she must enjoy conversation with youth and be able to relate well with them in order to communicate an understanding of Branch Groups.

The responsibilities of the leader include the following:

1. The leader must be a fully participating member of the group. Therefore she or he must be a person concerned about her or his own spiritual formation, a person who keeps the articles of the covenant just as the other members do.

2. The leader is responsible for keeping the group focused on its primary purpose, and for building discipleship through accountability to the disciplines.

3. The leader opens and closes the weekly meetings with prayer.

4. The leader is the "clock watcher," keeping the conversation flowing from member to member, clause to clause of the covenant, making sure that all have the opportunity to report.

Flow of conversation in a typical small group

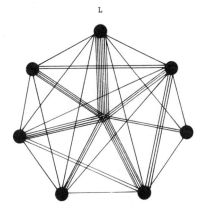

All of the members may interact, with the leader
playing a non-directive role.

Group dynamics can help with this responsibility. The conversation dynamics of a general sharing group might be diagrammed like this. Each circle is an individual member and each connecting line represents conversation between individuals.

In such a group, conversation is rather freewheeling. Anyone and everyone may talk to anyone and everyone about anything. There is limited control over the direction of the conversation. Those who are naturally more talkative will dominate and careful listening depends upon the respectfulness of each member. There is no designated leader.

In the Branch Group, conversation flows primarily under the direction of the leader. The leader can greatly influence the mood and the agenda of the conversation. Members may talk to one another, but the leader can ensure that all receive equal attention and respect. The conversation of a Branch Group can be diagrammed like this:

Flow of conversation in a Covenant Discipleship Group

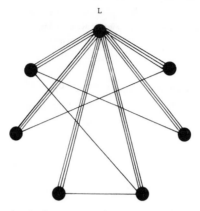

The catechetical process of accountability gives the
leader a directive role.

The Branch Group has a wagon wheel effect. The leader is clearly identifiable. The majority of the conversation flows from the leader to the other members of the group.

This diagram does not imply that reporting must always go rigidly around in the circle. The order of reporting may change. Someone may volunteer to share next. The leader must simply make sure that all have equal opportunity to participate.

5. The leader is responsible for the tone and dynamics of the group. The overwhelming feeling should be a positive and supportive one. The language used should reflect love rather than a rigid judging of obedience to the letter of the law. Again, these are not freewheeling, caring/ sharing sessions. The members are to follow Wesley's advice, "Watch over one another in love." The language of love is to express understanding, empathy, make supportive suggestions when appropriate, care for each other, and, whenever possible, celebrate victories and forgive failings. **At no time should insensitive, harsh, hurting words be tolerated.**

The leader may want to design a brief, informal ritual or expression for forgiveness and another for thanksgiving. Use them as appropriate for each member of the group. Remember that it is more important to rejoice over a member who has prayed four days than to condemn because of failure to pray on Thursday.

6. The leader will need to be sensitive to the specific needs of an individual. Offer to meet at special times with one or more individuals if there is a call for special support for one or more members. If one person is struggling in a particular way, invite the entire group to extend its meeting time for additional conversation. Do not skip the remaining reporting process in the covenant.

An adult leader has the responsibility for referring individual members to specific places of support if such is deemed beneficial. Leaders should be familiar with community resources such as school counselors, availability of the pastor, and other professionals.

7. State frequently the need for the group to respect the confidentiality of any particular situations discussed in the weekly meeting. Remember that to give an account, one may use general descriptions. If Jack is having a difficult experience with peer pressure, he need not share names and details unless he so chooses. As a leader, you may even discourage such detail if it gives occasion for gossiping.

8. The leader should be careful to encourage an appropriate level of commitment within the Branch Group. Not all young people can carry out this commitment with the same level of seriousness. Members of the group need to guard against a kind of phony solemnity. Being Christian needs to be experienced with a dose of laughter and enjoyment. Sometimes the situations in which we find ourselves encourage us to laugh at ourselves. We obviously do not laugh at another, but a little humor can help us step back and can give us a new perspective on ourselves, the situation, and life. Certainly we know a joyous God. On the other hand, make sure the group meetings are not taken so lightly that the group's commitment and accountability go unsupported and unrecognized.

9. The leader must recognize that progress will not come equally among all the members. For some youth, some clauses will come easily. For others, different clauses will be easier. In many cases the fruit of Branch Groups will depend primarily on the individual commitment of the members. Progress may be slow. Do not become discouraged or allow the members to become discouraged, if things seem to be improving slowly. Keep your expectations realistic. It is not the distance left between the present and the goal that matters. What counts most is whatever progress has been made. We must crawl and then take baby steps before we can run the marathon.

10. If, in spite of your best efforts, you find the group waning, ask these questions.

A. Have we lost sight of our purpose? Go back to the beginning and remember what it means to be a disciple and how Branch Groups can help.

B. Are we bogged down in legalism with the covenant? Talk about how the covenant is only a means to an end. The end is to open ourselves to God's grace.

C. Are we reporting in a perfunctory or rote manner? If the goal is to be open to God, begin as a group to ask questions about where you are experiencing the movement of God's grace. What have you learned or what are you learning about yourself and God? Take the emphasis off your own faithfulness and put it onto God and what God is doing through your faithfulness.

D. If you have been meeting for at least three months, maybe it is time to re-negotiate the covenant. If you have not been meeting for at least three months, consider the other options. To re-negotiate too quickly may simply be a way to avoid doing what you know you should do but would rather not do. If this is the case, a discussion of Paul's personal experience in Romans 7:15-25 may be helpful.

Remember that in the natural life cycle of any group, there are highs and lows. Sometimes the lows are great catalysts for huge strides forward. Be patient.

If nothing seems to be effective in moving a group off dead center, then ask the group to seriously evaluate their situation. If termination of the Branch Group appears to be the only solution, set up a specific process for ending the group. Have a closing group meeting, affirm the individual members, encourage them to pray for guidance as they consider other options for giving their discipleship attention, and invite them to join another Branch Group or some other group provided for the youth of your church. It is healthier for the group to initiate termination than to watch passively the dissolving of the group. Experiencing a group that slowly dies out and fades away can be very painful for the individual members.

11. The adult leader has the responsibility for the general public relations of Branch Groups in your church. Through articles in the church newsletter, conversation, and appropriate meetings, help parents, other youth not involved, and the congregation as a whole to understand what Branch Groups are all about.

Help people understand that Branch Groups are not cliquish or exclusive. New persons interested in Branch Groups must always feel included and welcomed. The process for including new members is addressed later. Branch Group members are not elitist or spiritually superior to those not in groups. In fact, they are in groups because of their weaknesses. They need the support of each other in order to be faithful disciples.

Guard against the temptation of arrogance on the part of the members of the Branch Groups. You are in the Branch Group because you need the help of others in keeping to the basics of your Christian discipleship. You are not there to judge whether others have the same need. God's grace works differently in each person's life. Just as you do not judge one another in the Branch Group, you are not to judge those not in a Branch Group.

12. Finally, and above all else, the leader has the responsibility for committing the entire Branch Group process and all of its members to God in prayer. Trust that if God has called you and your church to this model, God will provide the wisdom and strength to guide the Branch Groups.

Chapter Eight

Forming a Branch Group

Recruitment

It is now time to ask how we are to identify and encourage youth to participate in a Branch Group. Starting on the right foot is important for any group. The beginnings of the Branch Group are particularly critical.

The best recruitment will be done on an individual and personal level. This enables the description and explanation of Branch Groups to be made in language that is relevant for the person being addressed. It also allows for the invitation to be given in a way that speaks to that particular youth.

The most likely candidates for a Branch Group are those already sensitive to the challenges of living life as a Christian. Some of these youth, even many of these youth, may be persons who are not already involved in the various other youth activities offered by your church. They may be, on the other hand, youth who are, or have been, very involved and are looking for a new challenge.

In inviting youth to become a part of a Branch Group, effective communication is of the utmost importance. Make sure that the terms used are well defined. Make sure that persons understand something about each of the following:

1. The meaning of discipleship
2. The role of disciplines of the faith as building blocks for discipleship
3. The concept of a covenant
4. The meaning of accountability as the agenda for a Branch Group

Remember that these words do not speak for themselves. They are

40

frightening words even to many adults. Discuss them in as nonthreatening language as is possible. Use examples to make them clear. Think about some of the images used in this manual. Speak about issues that are relevant for the person to whom you are offering the invitation. It is a personal invitation. Do not hesitate to emphasize the benefits of, as well as the commitment to, the Branch Group.

In giving the invitation, remind persons that Jesus called the first disciples with a simple, "Follow me." They need to prayerfully consider if this is something they believe that God would like them to do right now. Their curiosity, their desire, maybe just their gut-level knowing will be the way God calls them. A call need not be a mysterious thing. The very invitation issued may be a call. Persons who say "yes" to Branch Groups should understand it as a call.

When recruiting, be specific with regard to the time commitment. Remember that the initial commitment is for twelve weeks. Then the group may recommit for additional time.

For public relations, offer an open invitation to all the youth in the church. Ask anyone interested to contact you, the leader. This is important because there may be someone who is really interested and ready for a Branch Group whom you have not considered. (God does work in mysterious ways.) Second, you want the image of inclusiveness right from the very beginning.

It is strongly recommended that you begin only one Branch Group initially. At the end of their introductory experience the members can help you discuss the Branch Group model with the other youth. As the initial group prepares for re-covenanting, another new group might be begun. At this time you may also need to recruit additional adult leaders for the new groups.

Should many youth express interest and you find you must begin more than one initial group, you will probably want a different adult leader for each group. This is not only in the interest of time and energy for the adults involved but also for enthusiasm and freshness in sharing. Adult leaders are full and regular participants, too.

Remember, each Branch Group is to consist ideally of six to eight youth and one adult leader.

Suggestions for Strategies

There may be better times than others in the life of your church's ministry with youth for the beginning of a Branch Group. Maybe Lent is a natural time to begin. Possibly it is part of the new fall programming in September. Youth may be particularly receptive to Branch Groups after a youth weekend retreat.

"Chrysalis" is the youth version of our denomination's adult experience, "The Walk to Emmaus." If "Chrysalis" is active in your area, Branch Groups may begin immediately after participation in one of their weekend experiences. A Branch Group may choose to begin its time together with a weekend retreat or by attending a "Chrysalis" weekend together.

Recruiting Branch Group members is a lot like picking fruit. The fruit is best when ripened on the vine. If you rush things and pick too early, the fruit does not ripen properly. If you wait too long, the fruit can literally rot on the vine. Pray for discernment. Some youth may be ready now. You may have to wait a little while and nurture some persons along before they are ready to make the commitment to Branch Groups.

Certainly not every young person in a congregation will want to belong to a Branch Group. Not every adult in a congregation desires participation in a Covenant Discipleship Group. In Jesus' day, crowds followed for miracles and teachings, but only a few became disciples. Jesus sent out only 72 from those crowds. (See Luke 10:1 ff.)

For John Wesley there was an understanding of the difference between **ecclesiola** (the little church) and **ecclesia** (the big church). Wesley resisted separating the Methodist Movement from the Church of England. The Church of England or the big church was the visible church that would root the Methodist Movement, or the little church, in the mainstream of the Christian tradition.

The United Methodist Church is the big church today. It is a large, pluralistic, inclusive church offering a variety of programs and ministries to persons, regardless of age, status, and experience. Like much of Jesus' ministry, The United Methodist Church brings a relevant message to a diverse crowd of people.

There is, however, a need today for the recurrence of the little church. Just as the class meeting of Wesley's day provided additional instruction, nurture, and fellowship for the early Methodists, so do we need Branch Groups for the youth of the large church today.

The little church and the big church both offer important and unique opportunities for Christians. They need each other. By appreciating their uniqueness and their significance, we can understand why some will participate in the Branch Group while others will not.

Organizing

Determine when and where the Branch Group will meet. Be specific about the length of the weekly meeting (60 or 90 minutes). Agree to the same time each week which is available for the members. This can be evening, after school, at breakfast, or before Sunday fellowship. Select a regular meeting place. This is best in the church, as distractions will be limited. The room should be warm and friendly. Persons will want to sit comfortably in a circle or around a table.

The First Meeting

It is important to begin the first meeting with a small informal time of worship. During this time, dedicate the Branch Group and its members to the grace of God. This affirms the sense of call for the individuals to the Branch Group.

The first task of the group will be to write together a mutually agreeable covenant. Beginning groups should stay close to the sample covenant. Rewrite the covenant (preamble and conclusion, too) enough so that the covenant is in words which hold meaning for the members. This process may actually take a few weeks. As specific clauses reach agreement, members are held accountable for them. Gradually the group builds to agreement and accountability for the entire covenant. Make sure each required core clause is represented.

It is possible to begin the Branch Group process with a retreat. In one weekend retreat, the service of dedication, the establishment of most of the covenant, and some of the following information for the first meetings together can be accomplished.

The Initial Twelve Weeks

The first twelve weeks in the life of a Branch Group are essential for understanding the importance of the Branch Group's working principles. It is also during this period that individual Bible study, prayer directives, and discussions at the weekly meetings can educate the youth about the importance of the core clauses. Remember that these core clauses are rooted in the means of grace and the works of mercy (doing good and avoiding harm) as developed by John Wesley for the early Methodist class meetings. These first twelve weeks are a time for discovering the building blocks of discipleship and becoming familiar with the process of reporting faithfulness to the clauses as accountability is experienced.

The adult leader will want to use the suggestions in the Appendix to make selections for assigned Bible readings. These selections should relate to the topic to be explored that week in the Branch Group meeting. Topics should be selected by taking into consideration what the members already understand and what they need to further understand for the Branch Group model to be effective.

Suggested topics include:

1. What is a disciple?
2. Why and/or how do we study the Bible?
3. Why is worship important?
4. What is the significance of a covenant?
5. What are the biblical roots and understanding of accountability within the community of faith?
6. What is Christian service?
7. What is the significance of avoiding harm?
8. What is Christian fellowship?
9. What does it mean to have Christ in us?

Design other questions and select your own scriptures that are helpful for the members of your Branch Group.

To keep the Branch Groups inclusive, you should invite new persons to participate. Those new persons will benefit from the reading and studying of this initial informational material.

Advanced Branch Groups

An advanced Branch Group is one where all the members have experienced the guidance of the initial twelve weeks. The members have committed for an extended period of time as a Branch Group.

Possibly the group has agreed to add further optional clauses. A few suggestions were made in Chapter 5 on "The Covenant."

Even for advanced groups, suggested lectionary readings for Bible study should be made by the leader and agreed to by the group. It is best if, in individual daily devotions, the members are studying the same scripture passages. Possibly the group will agree to a common study guide.

Some groups may express interest in a common service project. Certainly if God is leading the group in this direction, they should obey. Be careful never to lose the primary focus of the Branch Group. There is no substitute for practicing the basic disciplines.

A group that agrees to renew its covenant beyond the initial twelve-week period may decide to take on a special emphasis. They may decide to learn about the meaning of justice and righteousness, or to learn about journaling, or to identify and work on a common service project, and so on. The youth should be encouraged to be creative.

Theoretically, the same Branch Group can exist indefinitely as long as they keep recommitting together for given periods of time, at least for three months and usually six to nine months. Advanced Branch Groups may also consist of different members as long as each person has experienced the initial twelve-week session.

Each time a group renews its covenant, the first meeting together should be some service of dedication. Their first task together is to revise and rewrite their covenant.

Let us turn now to the process of renewing the covenant.

Chapter Nine

Renewing the Covenant

Each covenant is for a specified period of time, at least three months. At the end of the specified time, the Branch Group is given the opportunity to recommit for an additional period of time and to make revisions to the present covenant.

There are several decisions facing the members of the Branch Group at this time. Each member must at this time decide if they will continue with a Branch Group. Will he or she stay in this same Branch Group, or if other groups are recommitting at this time, will he or she join another group? Those who choose to continue will need to prepare a new covenant and agree on the time period for this new covenant.

Evaluation

A time of evaluating the Branch Group should occur at the end of the agreed covenant period. This is a time to assess how the group is doing, to see the progress that has been made, to decide how the group will continue.

Several questions for reflection, if considered, may help individual members determine the quality of their involvement in the Branch Group. If they are considering termination or changing groups, these questions may help them make a responsible decision. These questions may also help the individuals determine a direction that would be beneficial for their next covenant.

The following questions are **personal questions for reflection** and may be best sent home for private use.

Personal Reflection

1. Have I carried out our covenant to the best of my ability, and have I been responsible in my accountability to God and the other members of the group?

2. What improvements in my Christian living have I experienced? Remember that even the very smallest advancements in faithfulness are significant to God.

3. God desires our best efforts. Have I given my best efforts to God in the Branch Group process? If not, what improvements can I make? Where do I still need improvement?

4. Have I experienced increased openness to the Holy Spirit and increased receptivity to God's grace? Think about specific examples.

5. What other activity or disciplines would help me develop spiritually and grow in my discipleship?

6. Is God calling me to continue to participate in a Branch Group at this time? Remember that we hear calls from God in a variety of ways. Sometimes we just know this is what we are to do. Sometimes God speaks to us through other people. Sometimes we trust our instincts and believe that what we desire is God's leading. One should engage in prayer about this question.

Evaluation Meeting

The Branch Group is to meet once after the covenant period for the sole purpose of evaluation. The first item on the agenda is the sharing of the individual answers to the last personal question for reflection. Will they continue in the Branch Group? The second agenda item is the *group evaluation* which is covered shortly. For now, here is a discussion of the possible situations that can emerge, depending on the decisions of the individuals to continue in a Branch Group.

Several options will emerge as individuals decide whether to continue in the Branch Group. The entire group may want to continue for an additional covenant period. Some persons may wish to continue but would like to join another group, provided there are others in existence. Some persons may wish to terminate the Branch Group altogether. An entire group may wish to terminate. Consider these situations one at a time.

A. A member chooses not to continue in any Branch Group. The group should design a meaningful way to say goodbye to the individual. Exiting a group should be done intentionally and with respect. A special conversation with the adult leader may be appropriate, to ensure that the decision to exit is for healthy reasons. Remind the person that such a decision should be made prayerfully.

Make sure that the person has not been hurt in some way. If he/she is leaving because the covenant was difficult to keep, remind the person that discipleship is not easy, but with practice it gets easier.

This may simply not be the right model for this person at this time in his or her life. It is essential that the person still feels affirmed as a valuable child of God.

B. An entire Branch Group is dissolving.
See the instructions given in Chapter 7 on "Leadership" for suggestions on terminating a group. Remember that it is better to officially end a group than to allow the members to experience the painful process of a group simply fizzling out.

Again, the adult leader should meet with the members, as a group or as individuals, and make sure that the exit is not for unhealthy reasons (such as too high expectations or simply taking the easy way out of a challenging situation). Stress the importance of prayerfully making this decision.

Remember that young persons often get involved in things to test or experiment and then discover that the involvement is not right for them. One of the benefits of the covenant renewal option is that it provides a way for an honorable exit. As with termination on the part of an individual, the termination of an entire group should still leave the individuals feeling affirmed as children of God. It is appropriate and even encouraged that these persons be encouraged to remain involved in other areas of the youth ministry of the church.

C. A member would like to join another Branch Group.
Again the adult leader should be in conversation with the person to make sure that there are no unhealthy undercurrents behind this decision. Rearranging groups will be discussed shortly.

D. Someone now wants to join this group. First, is there a vacancy? If yes, has the interested person already experienced the initial twelve-week session? If yes, then great care will have to be exercised in bringing new members into a group. Remember that the already existing group has a common history. Can they graciously make a new person feel included and welcomed?

The adult leader needs to assist the group in deciding if they are open to new persons. The final decision is to be made jointly between the adult and the youth members. The primary concern should be the feelings of the individuals. It may be easier to form several new groups, providing there are enough interested persons. New groups are particularly helpful if there are several persons who desire to change groups.

Changing the Membership

Remember that, although under many circumstances forming several new constellations of Branch Groups may be desirable, groups that have been cohesive may resist such changes. The judgment of the adult leader is important in balancing the benefits of a Branch Group that has become a close-knit unit, and the benefits of reshuffling members so as to include new persons more effectively.

Some will think that reshuffling periodically is important to ensure that the Branch Groups do not turn inward upon themselves and stagnate. There are other options for keeping a group on target. These options, if used properly, will leave reshuffling as a last resort. These options include refresher discussions using the material of the first twelve-week session, patience, and effective coaching by the leader.

If several Branch Groups are reforming their membership, it is suggested that all interested persons meet at the same time in a large room. Place several sheets of newsprint around the room. On each sheet place a different suggested time for a Branch Group to meet. Ask each person to sign the appropriate sheet for the time which suits his/her needs. A person may need to add and remove his or her name several times until a workable combination for each Branch Group has emerged.

If you have several Branch Groups and they can meet at the same time for their group evaluation sessions, then this reshuffling of membership can occur during the same meeting. Reshuffling should not occur, however, until the present groups have completed the following group evaluation.

Group Evaluation

At the evaluation meeting, after members share the results of their personal reflection, the second agenda item is the group evaluation. The Branch Group should, as a whole, examine and discuss questions, such as the following, which deal with the overall group process:

1. Which disciplines in the covenant have we followed most consistently?
2. Which disciplines have given us the most difficulty?
3. Do any of the clauses in our covenant need to be reworded to achieve stronger emphasis, direction, or clarification?
4. Do we wish to add any optional clauses to the already existing necessary core clauses?
5. If your covenant includes more than the required core clauses, are the requirements of your covenant realistically attainable for the members of the group?
6. Has your group held each other accountable for their discipleship?
7. Has your conversation with one another during the reporting at the weekly meetings been helpful, positive, supportive, and loving?
8. Identify how your group has helped each other become more faithful disciples. How can you be more helpful?
9. Do you feel a need to review any of the material from the initial twelve-week session?
10. What are some issues or disciplines which have arisen during this covenant period that you would like to include in the new covenant?

Reorganizing

After completing the group evaluation time, the Branch Groups need to reorganize. The following decisions should be made:

1. Establish the membership of the Branch Group(s). They either remain mostly the same or you will have followed some procedure for reshuffling.

2. Agree to day, time, and length of time (60 or 90 minutes) for the weekly meeting.

3. Arrange the place for the weekly meeting.
4. Agree to the length of the renewal period.

You are encouraged to close this total evaluation event with some form of worship. It may be necessary to affirm those persons who are leaving Branch Groups. It should definitely affirm and dedicate the new Branch Groups. Revising John Wesley's Covenant Service may be particularly meaningful at this time.

New Members

An excellent way to encourage new persons to form beginning Branch Groups is to invite them to a time of sharing with persons already in groups. A time for fellowship around a meal and then an invitation to several Branch Group members to talk about their experiences often excites new persons to join.

Such a fellowship time could easily occur immediately following the time of evaluation and reorganization. It could even be on the same day.

Remember, though, that these new persons should form separate groups and begin with the introductory twelve-week session material.

Writing the New Covenant

The first task of a reorganized Branch Group is to agree again to a group covenant. Using the information from the above questions and the resulting evaluation discussion, your Branch Group must now rewrite its covenant for the renewed time period. Do not forget that the required core clauses covered in the suggested sample covenant must **always** be a part of a Branch Group's covenant in order for the model to be effective.

Maybe the Branch Group will want a specific emphasis for its time together. Will all the members be learning about journaling as a discipline? Is the group concentrating on increased sensitivities to injustice and ways to work against it? Are members reading additional material daily about prayer life? Maybe the group has decided to educate others about world hunger. No special emphasis is required, and the core clauses can never be overlooked, but give the Branch Groups the freedom of creativity.

Once again, depending upon the time of year and desire of the group, a renewed covenant should be for at least three months, and six to nine months is most beneficial. At the end of that time, the above process of evaluation and rewriting occurs again. The cycle continues as long as the Branch Group remains a group.

Retreat Setting

A retreat setting may be an ideal place to ask the above questions, to form the new Branch Groups (if there are to be any), and to actually write the new revised covenant(s). The following agenda items might be helpful for sessions:

Session 1. Personal evaluation. Participants may reflect prayerfully on the personal questions in private, and then have some time for sharing in their Branch Group. As a leader, you may find it beneficial to ask persons to respond in writing. The only response that would be shared with the Branch Group at this time is whether or not they desire to remain a part of a Branch Group.

Session 2 might deal with the concept of "call" as it relates to the Branch Group.

Session 3 would be the opportunity for the present Branch Groups to spend time with the group evaluation questions.

Session 4, if there are several Branch Groups present, can be devoted to the process of reorganizing the groups. This is particularly important if it is necessary to do major reshuffling in the membership constellations of the groups. If the membership of the groups is remaining primarily the same, this session is about defining the new time, day, and place for the weekly meeting, and the length of commitment for the new period.

A **final session** can provide time for the reorganized Branch Groups to begin the covenant writing process. What changes and additions will they make, if any?

It is even possible to invite interested persons who never have been in a Branch Group to come along and learn. These persons can ·spend some sessions with some of the introductory information used in the first twelve-week cycle of any Branch Group.

The retreat might have a **closing worship,** using Wesley's Covenant Service (for examples see the *Covenant Discipleship Quarterly,* January 1986, p. 3).

Branch Group Overview

Recruit members—six to eight youth and one adult.
The initial twelve-week session
> Determine when, how long (60 or 90 minutes), and where to meet.
> Dedicate the members and the process with informal worship at the first meeting.
> The first task together is to write and agree to a covenant in your own words similar to the sample covenant.
> Sign the covenant.
> Through the twelve weeks
>> —Conduct regular Branch Group meetings, including the use of reporting individually for the purpose of accountability.
>> —Study topics which educate members about the dynamic of the Branch Group and the disciplines of the core clauses.
>> —For use in the personal devotional daily time, assign recommended Bible passages and prayer suggestions.

End with evaluation, and personal reflection on the group experience.

Reorganize
> One of the following options is apparent.
> 1. The Branch Group remains the same and re-covenants.
> 2. A new Branch Group is formed and begins the initial session.

Eventually there may be more than one advanced Branch Group (Advanced members have completed the initial session.)
> 3. These groups remain relatively stable in membership and simply agree to new covenants.
> 4. There may be reshuffling of the membership of the advanced groups followed by covenant writing.
> 5. After establishing the membership of the group, determine day, time, place for weekly meeting (including specifying the length of

the meeting, 60 or 90 minutes) and length of commitment for the re-covenanting period (at least three months, preferably six to nine months).

6. Rededicate the members and the process with informal worship.

Re-commit

Write and agree to revised covenant.

Optional clauses may be added, but the core clauses are absolutely necessary.

End this session with evaluation as well.

Reorganizing and re-committing for the advanced groups can occur as many times as the group desires to be in existence.

All new Branch Groups must experience the material of the twelve-week initial session.

Chapter Ten

Branch Groups and the Congregation

What is the relationship of the Branch Group to your congregation? This is an important question as the visibility of Branch Groups increases in your congregation.

John Wesley had no intention of creating a new denomination with the Methodist Movement. Wesley wanted to provide a small church in the big Church of England. The Methodist Movement needed the Church of England.

The first element of the relationship between Branch Groups and the local church is that the Branch Groups are dependent on the larger community. It is in the larger community that worship is performed, avenues emerge for Christian outreach, instruction occurs, fellowship in the broadest sense is felt, and the needs of the world and the message of the gospel converge.

Second, you might ask if the larger church really needs the smaller church. For Wesley, the answer was "yes." He hoped that the Methodist Movement would revitalize and bring new energy to the Church of England.

What about today? Do Branch Groups benefit the entire church? We know there are certainly many personal benefits for those who are members of Branch Groups. When being a Christian in this world gives us bumps and bruises, we receive comfort and are supported by the other members. To meet the difficult challenges of life, we are becoming strong in the faith and learning habits that will sustain each of us throughout our lives. God sometimes seems closer if for no other reason than that we are paying more attention to God.

Wesley used the image of the muscle. The large church is like the human body. It is made up of many parts, all of which are important and necessary for the body to be the body. Wesley hoped that the early class meetings of the Methodist Movement would be the church's muscle. As such, it needed discipline and exercise—the regular practice of using the

55

means of grace and doing works of mercy. Just as a body that is all muscle cannot live, we need blood and tissue and organs; so is it important to affirm those in the larger church who are not part of the muscle. The larger church needs the muscle, though, to move and strengthen the church.

Branch Groups can benefit the larger congregation by being muscle for the church. Do not press the image too far, as we would not want to say that the only muscle of a congregation is its Branch Groups. We do want persons to understand, that to strengthen the discipleship of any of a church's membership, youth included, we strengthen the effectiveness for ministry of that entire congregation.

Another vivid image from scripture is that of leaven in the loaf. The leaven is the yeast which makes bread rise. The youth of Branch Groups can be leaven in the loaf of the church. Only God knows what the results of this leaven at work will be. Don't be surprised if Branch Groups begin to plant seeds and challenge the church to increase its involvement in mission and ministry in new and dynamic ways.

The third issue in the relationship between Branch Groups and the local church is the key issue of any relationship, communication. Many parents and other concerned adults may wonder what your Branch Group is all about. Communication about the purpose and process of the Branch Group model will be very important.

If there are Covenant Groups in your church using the model of Covenant Discipleship, it is sufficient to say that a Branch Group is a youth version of adult covenant groups. If your church does not have Covenant Groups, then several things may need to be explained.

Branch Groups should be seen as small groups that allow youth to help each other live more faithful Christian lives. Share some of the issues that are discussed, such as the meaning of discipleship, which is demonstrated by the disciplines of regular worship, daily prayer and Bible reading, setting a Christian example in everyday life, and service to others.

Let the congregation know that these groups do not just teach about these disciplines. The members have covenanted together to practice these disciplines. The youth are learning by living these vital building blocks of the faith. In so doing, Branch Groups are helping form dedicated and committed Christians for leadership in the church of tomorrow.

Some adults may not understand the accountability process. Help them to understand that the weekly meeting is a place for reporting the successes and the failures of the previous week. It is an occasion for support and understanding. The youth are not about harshly judging or criticizing one another. They are experiencing Christian fellowship in its purest sense. They are discovering that they are not the only ones struggling with what it means to follow Jesus truly.

Most of all, it is important that adults and members understand that Branch Groups are not for everyone. Those in Branch Groups are not better than other youth, more mature, or more Christian. The groups are not elitist. Branch Groups involve youth who have recognized their need for working out their faith in the context of a small community of believers. Here they may talk frankly about the issues of discipleship and learn from experience.

Communicating effectively about Branch Groups will strengthen the relationship between the groups and the church. The adults of the congregation may take pride in the commitment of their young people.

The truly unique characteristic of the Branch Group is that it holds benefits for both the individual participant and the church. Many, in fact most, small group options in the church today are primarily for the growth of the individual. Yes, individual discipleship is enhanced, but by definition and design, Branch Groups are rooted in the church. We cannot be disciples without being in community. The strength of the relationship between the Branch Group and the local church is that they are mutually beneficial. Branch Groups empower youth to assist the entire church in being the church of Jesus Christ.

Chapter Eleven

Commonly Asked Questions

This manual supplies the necessary information for the beginning and sustaining of Branch Groups in the church. The following are the top 25 miscellaneous questions frequently asked.

1. What if one member of the Branch Group is a chronic non-attender at the weekly meetings? This problem should be handled individually. Part of the covenant is to be present at the meetings for the purpose of engaging in Christian fellowship. The group, and specifically the leader, has the responsibility of holding the individual accountable for this commitment. If the individual's attendance is left unaddressed, the nonverbal message to the other Branch Group members is that the commitment is not really important.

The missing member needs to know that the group cares enough to let the person know he or she is missed. Sometimes non-attendance is a way of seeking attention. Sometimes it is because of a difficulty in one's personal life. Sometimes it is because of unavoidable conflicts. The individual needs the understanding, encouragement, and support of the group. Care should be expressed. There is a fine line between gentle nudgings and hassling, so be sensitive.

2. What if a person knows he/she must miss one meeting due to some temporary scheduling conflict? Such conflicts are a natural part of life. It is the individual's responsibility to let the group know, preferably in advance, if they are not attending this week.

3. What if an individual desires termination before the end of the agreed covenant period? Again this should be handled individually to determine the reasons for such a desire. If there is no option but for the individual to break the covenant, encourage him or her to explain this to the group. Above all else, the exit should be with honor and affirmation of the worth of the individual. Certainly the person has struggled over this decision, and his or her decision is to be respected.

4. Can a person drop out of a Branch Group and then reenter later? Yes. Follow the instructions for adding a member to a group. Does the person need a "refresher course" on any of the introductory material?

5. How long does it take for a group to develop cohesiveness? The variable here is how well the youth knew each other before entering the Branch Group. In many instances, the group may just begin to feel comfortable and close as they end the initial twelve-week period. Another factor is how open the conversation is during the weekly meetings. Sometimes one open and talkative youth will serve as a catalyst for the group's progress. One needs to be patient.

6. What if the group suffers from boring, rote responses in the reporting process? This is normal in the beginning as members become familiar with the process. By asking leading questions the group can move beyond this. "Are you experiencing any difference between the days when you pray and when you do not? Can you tell us about it?" Obviously using the topical suggestions for the first twelve weeks may break the ice.

7. What about guilt from breaking the covenant? Some guilt is healthy and some is out of proportion for the "violation." Grace is about forgiveness that wipes away guilt and enables new beginnings. Members might find it helpful to learn that healthy guilt is a great motivator of change. The best way to deal with guilt is to avoid causing the need for it in the first place. Sometimes the temptation is to lower the expectations in order to alleviate the uncomfortable guilt. If expectations for the process and one's self are realistic, and there is a commitment to the goal, then this temptation can be avoided.

8. What if one person is disruptive? There is usually a reason for this. Handle it personally and be sensitive.

9. What if the group does not seem to be taking the process seriously? Remember that risking for improved discipleship is difficult. Humor serves its purpose well as a defense mechanism. Give the group a chance to feel secure. Be patient. Sometimes one of the youth will eventually challenge the group to move ahead. The leader can gently nudge. Over a few weeks, lovingly increase the nudgings to a challenge, but avoid condemnation. Being too demanding could further threaten the group's security with one another. Keep your expectations realistic.

10. What can be done if the members cannot remember what has happened during the week? Accurate recalling is an important part of reporting at the weekly meeting. Some find it helpful to use a calendar and jot down each day where they were faithful. They can even record significant events of the day. Be creative.

11. Should journaling be encouraged? Journaling is often considered a spiritual discipline. The benefits are enormous. It also requires additional time. Most youth are comfortable journaling two or three times a week. It can focus on intentionality in prayer, study, and personal improvement. It can serve as a yardstick for measuring improvement as present entries are compared to past ones. Journaling should be viewed as personal and as such, the quality of writing skills is inconsequential. It is helpful, but is not for everyone. If journaling is used, teach some basics so as to make it less threatening.

12. What about parents? Their support is important for affirmation and practical considerations such as transportation to a meeting. Help them to understand the purpose and design of Branch Groups.

13. What if someone joins a Branch Group because of parental pressure? Discuss this with the parents so that they understand why this group is not for all youth. It should be the decision of the youth to join a group. If a youth is not interested and the parent wants him/her to be, help the parent understand that there is nothing wrong or abnormal about their youth's lack of interest.

14. What if someone joins because of peer pressure? Peer pressure is usually used in a negative way. It can, however, be a positive thing. It may bring someone into a group, but it may not provide the depth of commitment to sustain the decision.

15. What is the role of the pastor? In some instances the adult leader may be the pastor. If not, the pastor's support and understanding are essential. He or she will be instrumental in communicating the concept of Branch Groups to the entire congregation. The pastor may be a pivotal point in the relationship between Branch Groups and the church.

Visits by the pastor to Branch Group meetings can be helpful. Serving the sacrament of Holy Communion, occasionally or regularly to a group during a weekly meeting, could actually become a part of a group's covenant.

16. How small can a Branch Group be? The optimum size is six to eight youth and one adult. To have a group of fewer than four youth and one adult is difficult. It depends on the particular individuals involved. In a group of fewer than six youth and one adult, adjust the length of time for the weekly meeting accordingly.

17. What if fewer than four youth are interested? In the small membership church, maybe there are more adults who will join with these youth and form a combination Branch Group-Covenant Discipleship Group. This option only requires that the youth and the adults are comfortable entering this adventure together. The youth and the adults need to treat one another equally.

18. How large can a group be? If the group has more than eight youth and one adult, patient listening to each other may be difficult. A group that is too large increases the risk for disruptiveness. It may be advisable to have two small groups rather than one large group.

19. Is the energy required for leading Branch Groups good stewardship of time when not all youth will be involved? A good shepherd goes after the one lost sheep. Remember the image of leaven in the loaf. Caring for one another in this group may have more far-reaching effects in the long run than many large gatherings.

20. Aren't we all too busy now? Everyone must set priorities and sometimes they are established by default. What is really important? There is enough time for what we really want to do in life. The time spent in these disciplines often makes the rest of the time one uses more productive.

21. Church programs come and go; is this another fad? Branch Groups are not another program and should not be viewed as such. The Branch Group is not a gimmick. It is a vehicle that facilitates the church in doing precisely the basic thing the church is called to do—develop and nurture discipleship.

22. How diverse can a group be? Extremely pluralistic. Adult Covenant Discipleship attracts persons across the theological spectrum. Those with a strong personal faith are challenged for social action. Those socially involved are challenged to find the resources of energy and power in a personal faith. The basic disciplines are the same for all Christians. The core clauses of the covenant speak to that which is the basis of Christian unity, openness to the grace of God. This can be true for youth as well.

23. Is this too legalistic? Granted there is often a fine line between practicing disciplines and rigid good works. Branch Groups are only legalistic if we forget the "why." This is only a means to an end and the end is not following the law but rather, availability to the movement of the grace of God.

24. Are these youth "normal"? Normal by what standards? The depth and level of interest on the part of youth today may be surprising. For years the church has been telling youth to pray, read the Bible, worship, serve, and be involved in fellowship with other Christians. How many of our youth are frustrated by being given expectations without being taught how to meet those expectations! Branch Groups are serious about the "how."

25. Does faithfulness ever become easy? Even the saints experienced dry spells written of as "desert experiences." They nonetheless strove for consistency in their disciplines. It may never be easy, but hopefully Branch Groups help to make it easier.

Chapter Twelve

Discerning Effectiveness

We have become a goal-oriented society. We chart results constantly. For our youth, this is particularly true since their life is about grades and report cards, winning competitions, rankings compared to others, and even detailed statistical records of wins and losses and averages in whatever sport they are involved.

Measuring effectiveness has become a great challenge for many churches. Measurable goals for ministry are not easy to write. So much of ministry seems intangible. Nonetheless, this manual would be incomplete without a few concluding thoughts about what one can expect if Branch Groups are effective. Sometimes we feel we have failed because our expectations were too high. We are not called to success, we are called to faithfulness. What are some realistic expectations for the results of effective Branch Groups? How will we know that Branch Groups are serving as effective vehicles for the development of discipleship?

With boldness, the following are realistic expectations of what may begin to occur if the Branch Group is effective. It may take some discernment to identify these signs when they appear amidst the particulars of each unique setting. Not all may occur for every group. In fact, if only one occurs, there is still effectiveness.

1. Participants are beginning to understand and appreciate the significance of practicing spiritual disciplines as building blocks for discipleship.

2. Participants are learning a language of faith that is their own as they share in the reporting process of Branch Groups.

3. There is increased interest and enthusiasm about issues of faith, particularly as they relate to how one lives daily.

4. Participants are asking questions, tough questions about faith. Finding answers will take a lifetime. Asking the questions is the important sign.

63

5. The group is beginning to jell into a cohesive unit where significant relationships within the community of faith can be experienced.

6. Rather than treating all youth as though they are alike, individuals are being nurtured and there are hints, maybe even strong evidence, of personal maturing.

7. Connections are being made between religion and real life, faith and service, being the church and caring for the world.

8. Conversation has moved from chit-chat to feelings and thoughts. The content of the conversation is sometimes about the awareness of God, sensitivity to God's involvement in life to prompt faithfulness, sensitivity to the experience of others around us and the needs of the world.

9. Participants are discovering that they are not alone. They have the support, acceptance, and understanding of other Christians. As well as unique differences, they are discovering that they have similar joys and concerns. Above all else, God is with them.

10. Participants are also discovering that there are resources beyond their own to assist them in meeting the challenges of life. Being open to God is about being open to the comfort, strength, and power that enhances life.

Branch Groups are not just another nice program for youth. Those who will decide to introduce Branch Groups must believe that they are giving these youth the necessary tools for being Christian. The most effective thing Branch Groups may do is plant valuable seeds, the fruits of which may not be evident for years. For those adults who lead, they may never know or see the fruits, but they are called to believe.

The effectiveness of the Branch Groups cannot be owned by human hands. The results ultimately belong to God. There is much that can be done to enhance effectiveness, but it cannot be manipulated for success.

Finally, Branch Groups are not about being prefect. Ever so slowly but steadfastly, they are about "going on to perfection."

Appendix A
Bible Readings

Suggestions for First Twelve Weeks

In the beginning, it may be best to start by assigning Bible selections to be read. The leader needs to decide whether the Branch Group needs specific verses assigned for each day. If so, a series of seven readings can be used each week. Perhaps members will need only four selections assigned for the week and can select on their own the other three readings.

The first twelve-week session is crucial for the life of the Branch Group. It is suggested that, for each week, the leader select a topic around which to build the readings. This will provide structure and help educate the members about the important concepts undergirding the entire process of the Branch Group. Select the topic for the week and decide which and how many passages will be assigned. The leader should feel free to tailor the topics to his or her specific group of young people. Perhaps the initial group will have agreed to meet for a 90-minute period. There can be group discussion at the weekly meeting regarding the readings for the week.

Using these passages will help orient the group to scriptural bases for Branch Groups before moving to a more general format. After the first twelve-week session, an advanced group may choose to continue using suggested passages selected by the leader. Some advanced groups may decide to study a particular book as the basis for their daily Bible reading. Some groups may choose a Common Lectionary to follow. In congregations where the lectionary is used, this will help the Branch Group discipline and enhance the worship opportunities for members. Most Branch Groups will always need some suggestions in regard to daily devotions. Just telling each other to read the Bible each day is not enough.

Scripture Readings for Branch Groups

COVENANT
 Genesis 9:1-17   Jeremiah 50:5-7
 Genesis 17:1-14   Jeremiah 31:31-34
 2 Chronicles 15:1-15   Hebrews 10:15-25

ACCOUNTABILITY/RESPONSIBILITY
 Psalm 144   Romans 14:12-23
 Matthew 12:36-37   1 Corinthians 8:7-13
 Acts 5:27-32   1 Peter 3:13-18
 Acts 20:32-36   James 5:16
                                    1 John 4:7-16

DISCIPLES/DISCIPLESHIP
 Psalm 63   Luke 14:25-33
 Isaiah 51:1-4   John 8:31-36
 Mark 8:34-38   John 12:24-26
 Luke 9:1-6   John 13:34-35
 Luke 9:23-26   John 17:24-26
 Luke 9:57-62   1 Timothy 6:11-15
 Luke 10:1-12

PRAYER
 Matthew 6:5-18   1 Kings 19:9-12
 Luke 11:5-13   Psalm 46
 Romans 8:26-28   Psalm 62
 Philippians 4:4-9   1 Thessalonians 5:16-18
 1 Timothy 2:1

SERVICE
 Matthew 10:29-37   Luke 10:29-37
 Matthew 25:1-13   John 13:1-20
 Matthew 25:14-30   2 Corinthians 5:16-6:2
 Matthew 25:31-46   James 2

BIBLE STUDY
 Psalm 119

WORSHIP
Psalm 96
Psalm 100

Psalm 111

FELLOWSHIP OF THE BODY
Psalm 133
Romans 12
1 Corinthians 12

Galatians 5:22-6:5
Ephesians 4:1-16

BRANCHES
Isaiah 11:1-10

John 15:1-15

OTHER POSSIBILITIES
Psalm 139
Matthew 5:1-16
Matthew 7:1-5
John 14

John 15:12-27
Romans 7:15-25
Galatians 3:28-29

Appendix B

Resources for Prayer

Most persons need help structuring their prayers. Most prayers are conversation about the day's happenings, personal requests, etc. It may be important to help youth learn to give God adoration, make confessions, offer thanksgiving, and make supplications or requests on behalf of others and themselves.

The following is a list of suggestions that will help persons widen the scope of their prayers. The purpose is to prevent group participants from falling into a rut with their prayers.

The leader may want to make a prayer suggestion for each day. The leader will want to make decisions about pacing the group with its prayer schedule. The leader will need a knowledge of the group's abilities. Maybe there is someone in the group who would like to write prayers for the youth to use in their devotional time. Do not feel bound by the list provided. Encourage one another to pray about the details of their own lives. The leader, or one of the youth, may write his/her own one-line suggestions. Finally, introduce them to prayers that are about silence and meditation. Begin teaching them to listen.

Two resources available from The Upper Room have been helpful for others in working with groups about their prayer lives. One is the *Workbook on Living Prayer* and the other is the *Workbook on Intercessory Prayer,* both by Maxie Dunnam.

Prayer Suggestions

1. Pray for the other members of my Branch Group.
2. Pray for people who are homeless.
3. Pray for the members of my family.
4. Pray for someone with whom I have had a disagreement.
5. Pray for people who are hungry.

6. Pray for time to be quiet and think about God.
7. Pray for patience with others.
8. Pray for the fulfillment of the covenant clauses.
9. Pray for the spiritual leaders in my church.
10. Pray for national and international leaders who negotiate nuclear arms.
11. Pray for persons who are unemployed.
12. Pray for my friends who face peer pressure in making moral decisions.
13. Pray for people who have no opportunity for education.
14. Pray for those who are victims of terrorism.
15. Pray for the families of terrorist victims.
16. Pray for the terrorists.
17. Pray for families in divorce situations.
18. Pray for those who live in war-torn lands and are afraid.
19. Pray for people who are working for peace in the world.
20. Pray for love and fellowship in my family.
21. Pray for someone who is sad and lonely.
22. Pray for someone I have seen excluded from friendship.
23. Pray for those who ridicule other persons.
24. Pray that I will know that God is near me.
25. Pray for illumination of the daily scripture readings.
26. Thank God for diversity among friends.
27. Pray for people who have life-threatening illnesses.
28. Thank God for the courage and example of persons with handicapping conditions.
29. Pray for people in prison and their families.
30. Pray that we may bring greater joy to those around us.
31. Pray for those who are ill.
32. Pray for a spirit of love in my family.
33. Pray for those who try to help others.
34. Pray for those who are addicted to drugs and alcohol.
35. Pray for those who are trying to stop their addictions.
36. Pray for strength to love family and friends even in disagreement.
37. Pray for teenagers who are parents.
38. Pray for those who are having trouble in school.
39. Pray for teenagers who have turned to crime.
40. Thank God for people who care for and work with troubled youth.

41. Pray for the ability to listen to God.
42. Thank God for the clergy and lay leadership in my church.
43. Thank God for the shared experiences of our Branch Group.
44. Thank God for the opportunities that come with each day.
45. Thank God for helping me to love and accept others who are different from me.
46. Thank God for chances to help someone in need.
47. Pray for the ability to love and accept myself.
48. Thank God for the person I am.
49. Pray for strength in resisting temptation.
50. Pray for courage to stand with my convictions under peer pressures.
51. Pray for courage, strength, and wisdom to challenge, and to be challenged.
52. Thank God for challenges that show me new things.
53. Pray for wisdom in relating to myself and others.
54. Thank God for those who teach me.
55. Thank God for someone who listens to me.
56. Thank God for those who give me guidance.
57. Pray for the ability to accept responsibility.
58. Pray for the ability to accept failure as part of life and the courage to try again.
59. Pray for help in listening to other people.
60. Thank God for friends' support when I'm sad and lonely.
61. Thank God that it's all right to grieve and feel badly when confronted with tragedy.
62. Thank God for God's love and support and grace.
63. Ask God some question about being Christian.
64. Share with God some of your hopes and dreams.
65. Share with God something you admire about who God is.
66. Share with God something that makes you angry.
67. Share with God why you are glad to be a Christian.
68. Pray for those suffering with AIDS.
69. Pray for those affected by apartheid.
70. Pray for people who live in oppressive countries.

Appendix C

A Daily Office

Many persons find it helpful to have structure for their daily devotional life. Youth may find the following particularly helpful for establishing a form for daily Bible reading and prayer.

1. OPENING PRAYER. A sentence prayer asking God to speak through scripture and reflection.

2. BIBLE READING. The passage suggested by the Branch Group Leader or assigned by a Common Lectionary.

3. REFLECTION TIME. Think about and possibly write about the answers to these questions.
   A. What was this passage about for the people of biblical times?
   B. What does the passage mean for us today?
   C. What is the passage saying to me right now?
   D. What am I going to do about what this is saying to me?

4. PRAYER TIME. Include thanksgivings, confessions, and requests for others and self. Use today's prayer suggestion.

5. CLOSING PRAYER. A sentence prayer asking God to help me carry the insights of this time throughout the day. Ask God to help me be aware of God's presence with me in all the moments of the day's activities.

Appendix D

Resources for Service

Service to a neighbor may be even more difficult than the other covenant clauses. While we know that the Christian is called to a life of service, we may need to teach each other ways in which service can be accomplished. Because of the diversity of life, it is not possible to compile a list of "Service to the Neighbor Acts" similar to the suggestions for daily Bible reading and prayer. Each Branch Group will need to discover the kinds of services that young people, individually and/or as a group, can render their neighbors. It may be helpful to study the parable of the good Samaritan (Luke 10:29-37). The thrust of the parable is the way in which Jesus turns the question "Who is my neighbor?" around so that it becomes "To whom am I to be a neighbor?" The answer is that we are to be neighbors to those who need mercy.

The parable of the good Samaritan teaches us that the good neighbor bound up real wounds with real bandages. A feeling of compassion is not enough. Love acts to remedy, to comfort, to support. The thirsty are given water; the hungry fed; the sick and the imprisoned are visited. Love does not give a prayer instead of food. Love may give a prayer with food, but the emphasis is on the food. This means that a good neighbor spends time and energy developing effective caring skills that serve needs.

Several years ago a survey was made asking people what other persons did in order to care for them. The consistent answers: "I was listened to." "The caring person heard what I was trying to say." One of the ways in which we care for and therefore serve and minister to others is to listen to what they are saying. The good neighbor accepts the responsibility for learning more about how to be a good neighbor. That means learning more about what hurts people and more about the situations and circumstances that cause hurt.

Christians must decide with whom to be a good neighbor, toward whom they will act in ministry, and what act they shall perform. There is risk in trying to help. There is the risk that you will not be welcomed, the risk that you may not really help, even the risk that you may hurt or injure. Faith is about being led to serve and having the courage and strength to take such risks.

Serving is often something persons do very privately and individually. Branch Groups should reinforce the "nice" things we do for others as significant. No act of kindness is too small. If a Branch Group is interested in something together, pray about what opportunities are available and go for where the group has sensitivities: visiting shut-ins, volunteering at hospitals or nursing homes, projects for hunger and mission, fund-raising for our denomination's Youth Service Fund, studying and getting involved in some social problem. The best resource to help with a total group project is available through and published by Discipleship Resources, entitled *Youth Servant Team Handbook.* This resource will show you how to organize a team of youth to enter the community and to do works of mercy for their neighbors.

Resource List

ACCOUNTABLE DISCIPLESHIP
Handbook for Covenant Discipleship Groups in the Congregation
This basic resource by David Lowes Watson provides the reader with essential historical and theological foundations of this early Methodist tradition, a step-by-step process by which to form CD groups, and its implications for ministry today. (order no. DR009B)

DISCIPULOS RESPONSABLES
Desarrollar Grupos de Discipulado Cristiano en la Iglesia Local
En este libro, el autor presenta una excelente base para la formación, desarrollo y acción de grupos de discipulos responsables en nuestra Iglesia. Por David L. Watson. Presentado por Mortimer Arias. (numero F023B)

THE EARLY METHODIST CLASS MEETING
Its Origins and Significance
Written by David Lowes Watson, this basic resource introduces the modern reader to the early Methodist class meeting. Guidelines for using the class meeting in local congregations are also offered. (order no. DR017B)

WESLEY SPEAKS ON CHRISTIAN VOCATION
From a theme of Christian vocation, Paul Wesley Chilcote has assembled selections from the literature by the Wesleys on "What do we teach?", "How do we teach?", and "What do we do?". Wesley speaks clearly to our turbulent times about doctrine, liturgy, worship, hunger, oppression, peace, and service in the world. Reflection questions follow each chapter. (order no. DR041B)

COVENANT DISCIPLESHIP BROCHURE
Explains the purpose and function of Covenant Discipleship groups. Available in sets of 100 only. Use as bulletin inserts and as "calling cards" for starting groups in your congregation. (order no. M298L)

COVENANT DISCIPLESHIP CONGREGATION KIT

Contains *Discovering the Modern Methodists* set of 2 videocassettes featuring David Lowes Watson, a vinyl 3-ring binder, a congregational guide, 8 issues of the *Covenant Discipleship Quarterly,* 1 copy of *Accountable Discipleship,* 1 copy of *The Early Methodist Class Meeting,* and 10 brochures to share with interested persons. (order no. M286P)

COVENANT DISCIPLESHIP MEMBER'S KIT

Contains 1 copy of *Accountable Discipleship,* 8 issues of *Covenant Discipleship Quarterly,* and a member's guide. (order no. M287P)

MATERIALS FOR GROWTH IN CHRISTIAN FAITH AND LIFE

P.O. Box 189 • Nashville. TN 37202 • Phone (615) 340-7285